What if you lost a pet?

If your pet wasn't in sight, you
might make a sign on a piece of
paper. Choose very bright colors.
Paint a picture and write your pet's
name. Place your sign where
everyone can see it.

What if you had a loose tooth?

If you could not chew, you could eat hot soup or bean stew with a spoon. Wait a few days and your tooth will come right out.

What if your old clothes did
not fit?

If you don't wear your old clothes and shoes, start with a box. Fill it up with your old things. Tie the box with string and bring it to a shelter.

What if you wanted to build
a birdhouse?

If you drew up a plan first, the
job would be smooth. A grown-up
could help you use tools. You could
place the birdhouse high in
a tree.

What if you had to clean your room?

You could make it a game and
pretend you are looking for clues
on a treasure map. You could look
over and under things. You might
find things you hadn't seen for a
long time!

What if you can't get to sleep
at night?

You might get a night-light in
your room. You might count sheep
or think of things you like. Soon
you will droop and fall asleep.